How
To Live
A
Life Of
Holiness

Malory Laurent

Contents

Dedication

To my amazing wife Mikerline, thank you for your unwavering support for more than two decades. To my sons Mike, Caleb, Daniel, and my daughter Hadassah, thank you for making me the father that I have become.

Foreword

We live in a time when human activities exert a significant influence on the environment in general. It is a time marked by apostasy, thrown into the deepest disarray. Therefore, drawing near to God is not just an option but rather a necessity.

In this perspective, Reverend Malory LAURENT, a man of God and pastor of the Salvation Church of God, is aware of the dizzying decline of the Christian faith and concerned with the exponential pace at which Satan is advancing its works in order to gain souls, offers us an excellent book entitled "HOW TO LIVE A LIFE OF HOLINESS."

This manual describes very clearly the importance of a holy life as well as the steps to achieve it. It presents the Holy Spirit as an indispensable agent of a sanctified life, a requirement made to all those who have chosen Jesus as their personal Savior. Throughout our existence, we must seek and practice the life of holiness on a daily basis.

I have been following the author for over a decade, and I can attest that sanctification has always been the focal point of his preaching. Furthermore, his ministry has always been influenced by a progressively sanctified life.

This book is, therefore, offered to all those who wish to live and flourish in a life of sanctification, which, according to the Bible, is the process by which a person devotes oneself to God and subsequently rejects sin. The rejection of sin itself does not happen at once. It is a progressive work that makes us more like Christ in our everyday actions.

My brothers and sisters in the Lord, I invite you to make this work a bedside book for your spiritual maturation, and I assure you that you will not regret it.

Reverend Renaud FENELUS

Introduction

"It is God's will that you should be sanctified..." (1 Thessalonians 4:3). This declaration of the apostle Paul in his first letter to the Christians of Thessalonica illustrates the importance of sanctification in the eyes of God.

The Bible says no one can separate us from the love of God that is revealed in Jesus Christ. God loves us eternally and wants to establish a deep and intimate relationship with each one of us. This is true for all of humanity, but even more so for the children of God. I am talking about those who have received Jesus as the personal Lord and Savior of their lives.

Nevertheless, it often happens that children of God go through spiritual deserts, moments when the relationship with God appears cold and distant. If many things can cause these deserts, we wish to consider one of the greatest among them: sanctification.

Sanctification and the Influence of the Church

Mankind lives in society. This is, in fact, the way he builds relationships with his peers. This society is as dynamic as the men who make it up. The practices of yesterday are not those of today, and today's values are not those of tomorrow.

Be it scientific progress, technological advances, or changes in morals, whatever the way in which change is brought within a society, it may be a powerful instrument of the devil.

Doesn't the Bible say that the whole world is under the power of the evil one? This is why the evolution of society contributes to further distancing humans from God and shapes them into a system of thought contrary to the principles of His Kingdom, even though that evolution is comprised of good things. Therefore, Christians of today must ensure that they do not merely reproduce the models that are offered by society.

Christians are, first and foremost, heavenly citizens who inhabit the earth temporarily. When a Christian agrees to reproduce the models that the world imposes on him, he ignores his primary mission in the world, which is to be a witness to Jesus Christ of Nazareth. Jesus said, "But you will receive power when the Holy Spirit comes on you; and you will be my witnesses in Jerusalem, and in all Judea and Samaria, and to the ends of the earth" (Acts 1:8).

To be a witness to Jesus is to carry His Word through the preaching of the gospel of salvation, but it is also to live the gospel. Hence, instead of being influenced by the world, Christians must instead influence others. That explains why the Bible commands Christians not to love this world or the things in it.

Yet today, the love of the world wins the hearts of Christians. The Word of God is often relegated to the background. This rejection of the Word leads to a lack of interest in sanctification, even among church leaders. Consequently, the Church has little influence on the world.

Sanctification and the Return of Jesus

Christians must be aware that the battles that take place on earth are, first and foremost, spiritual. We do not struggle "against flesh and blood, but against the rulers, against the authorities, against the powers of this dark world and against the spiritual forces of evil in the heavenly realms" (Ephesians 6:12). If governments go to war and pass immoral laws, for example, it is simply because they are led and influenced by these evil spirits.

Among the biggest struggles in the Church today are distraction and apostasy, which tools are increasingly being used by the devil. To do this, the devil leads Christians to focus on anything that can replace the true gospel. The Church is distracted by trivial things or doctrines that are contrary to the Holy One. Therefore, it is evident that the Church is not preparing for the return of Jesus.

Yet biblical prophecies are being accomplished. The Bible had already clarified through Daniel, who had seen in a dream 4 beasts, which would represent 4 kings of the earth (Daniel 7:3), that the end times would come with great difficulty for Christians. The fourth beast represents a fourth kingdom on earth, which shall be different from all the kingdoms; it shall devour the whole earth, trample it down, and break it to pieces (Daniel 7:23).

The sculpture donated to the Organization of the United Nations by the Government of Mexico and erected in front of the UN headquarters in New York in 2021 is strangely reminiscent of Daniel's vision. Indeed, in this vision, Daniel prophesies that we will witness the reign of the beast and its servants. Added to this are the prescriptions of the 25th verse of the same chapter, which affirm that "he will speak against the Most High and oppress his holy people and try to change the set times and the laws. The holy people will be delivered into his hands for a time, times and half a time he will speak words against the Most High."

The predictions of the prophet Daniel are now coming true. We must, therefore, also await the judgment predicted in the 26th verse of the same chapter.

Apostle John describes a similar scenario in the entire thirteenth chapter of the book of Revelation:

"The beast I saw resembled a leopard but had feet like those of a bear and a mouth like that of a lion. The dragon gave the beast his power and his throne and great authority" (Revelation 13:2).

In the seventh verse, it says, "It was given power to wage war against God's holy people and to conquer them. And it was given authority over every tribe, people, language, and nation."

This power, described with the higher authority of this beast, a symbol of the antichrist, over peoples, languages, and nations, brings to mind the biggest international organization in the world, the UN.

The prophet ends with a call to vigilance, stating, "Whoever has ears, let them hear" (Revelation 13:9). Christians must therefore be ready for the expected return of Christ.

Signs of the imminent return of Christ are also described in 2 Timothy 3:1-5.

The Bible tells us about selfishness, which is becoming more and more prevalent in defiance of the empathy shown by Jesus during His time on earth. Children are rebellious to the point of acting without restraint and respect for their parents. In this case, I cannot count how many times I have been called by parents who suffer from the mischief of their offspring.

I often witness a set of practices adopted by young girls who are members of Christian assemblies and who disregard the values advocated by Christian morality. They are sometimes members of the worship team or the ushering service, just to name a few. Despite an active presence in the ministry, some young women go on to live with men who could be their grandfathers, while others agree to be the mistresses of married men.

Because of my responsibilities as a leader at Salvation Church of God, I have had the privilege of privately discussing with young women who have confessed to me that they have been in love with married men. This testimony is symptomatic of a daily reality: even in church, it's mainly young women who have become indifferent to Christian morality.

I take this opportunity to point out that morality should be helpful in many ways—so helpful that it teaches us to be moderate in our words and actions. For instance, a moral person knows how to dress decently. A moral woman will never wear excessively tight skirts or dresses in public or shorts that reveal the full shape of her body. Similarly, a moral man will never wear pants that are too tight and/or tight-fitting shirts in public. A moral person does not commit adultery and never hits his or her spouse. Without having to be a Christian, a moral person cannot choose a minor as a fiancé, lover, or spouse, and certainly cannot be homosexual or zoophilic.

Yet, these immoral acts are sometimes committed by men and women who accept the Lord Jesus as their Savior. They are people who refuse to live a life of holiness.

The story of Joseph at Potiphar's house is the perfect example of morality. Potiphar's wife asked Joseph to sleep with her. What did Joseph do? The Bible says that "he refused and said to his master's wife, 'Behold, with me in charge, my master does not concern himself with anything in the house; everything he owns he has entrusted to my care'" (Genesis 39:8).

Joseph's position is, first and foremost, a moral one because he is aware of and grateful for everything Potiphar has done for him. Thus, he cannot sleep with his master's wife. Therefore, even when Christian considerations are excluded, anyone could have the same reaction as Joseph, plainly out of moral duty.

Verse 9 of the same chapter validates my thesis in the sense that Joseph told his master's wife, "No one is greater in this house than I am. My master has withheld nothing from me except you, because you are his wife. How then could I do **such a wicked thing** and **sin against God**?" I write part of the sentence in bold to draw your attention to the moral aspect that I am telling you about. Joseph used the word "wicked" to first show the moral aspect of the situation. The second part reveals the spiritual aspect of Joseph's position. Being moral is enough to know that one should not sleep with someone else's wife.

In this sense, some pagans are much more moral than people who call themselves Christians. Had morality been the only condition to receive the salvation of Jesus Christ, those pagans would be saved, while people who have accepted Jesus as their Savior are floundering in immorality. In fact, some societies are not Christian, but they are, to a certain extent, moral. Paradoxically, the culture of morality is diminishing in churches.

Furthermore, we are prone to overexposure to immorality. Whether through the traditional press or modern information and communication technologies, hardly a day goes by without at least one scene of immorality running in loops on these platforms. Consequently, more than ever, Christians need to live a life of holiness while setting themselves apart from these worldly practices.

Added to the previously mentioned morality crisis is a group of people who call themselves apostles, doctors, evangelists, pastors, and prophets without any calling from God. They are distancing His people from authentic faith. The emergence of the new trend of the gospel that I call "feel good" amounts to considerable progress in the devil's work. Whenever they pick up a microphone, this group of preachers aims to flatter the weakest souls.

I was shocked to hear a very popular pastor in the United States on a popular television show state that he does not address the notion of holiness in his sermons because he does not want to hurt the people of

God. To correctly understand his words, sanctification does more harm than good to the people of God. This leads us to the following question: how can the people who readily claim to be "God's people" refuse to practice His principles?

The preacher is not the author of the message. He must simply pass on the message assigned to him, as it was received, at his own risk of being hated. Did Jesus not say, "If the world hates you, know that it has hated me before it hated you" (John 15:18)? The Bible says in 2 Peter 1:21, "For prophecy never had its origin in the human will, but prophets, though human, spoke from God as they were carried along by the Holy Spirit."

It is, therefore, clear that the "feel good" preachers do not speak from God. While lacking anointing, they are representatives of Satan, the devil, whose job is to curb the spread of the gospel of salvation because the primary objective of the enemy remains to lead a considerable number of humans to Hell with him. Hence the importance of sanctification.

Definition and Typology of Sanctification

According to the translation of Larousse, an illustrious French dictionary, to sanctify comes from the vulgar Latin word *sanctificare*, from classical Latin *sanctus*, which means to make someone holy or to put a person in a state of grace.

In the biblical sense, the verb "to sanctify" comes from the Greek word *hagiasmos*, meaning to make holy, to consecrate, to separate from the world, to be set apart from sin so that we can have an intimate relationship with God and serve Him properly, especially with joy. 1 Thessalonians 5:23 says, "May God himself, the God of peace, sanctify you through and through. May your whole spirit, soul and body be kept blameless at the coming of our Lord Jesus Christ" (1 Thessalonians 5:23).

Notwithstanding the use of the verb "to sanctify," the criteria relating to sanctification are found in the Bible. The first criterion is the unconditional love of the living God. Jesus taught us to love God when he said, "Love the Lord your God with all your heart and with all your soul and with all your mind" (Matthew 22:37). The second criterion is the effort to be righteous while living a life of holiness. We find this condition in 1 Thessalonians 3:13: "May he strengthen your hearts so that you will be blameless and holy in the presence of our God and Father when our Lord Jesus comes with all his holy ones."

We must also practice charity coming from a heart where purity is cultivated, demonstrate good conscience, and have a sincere and unshakable faith (1 Timothy 1:5). Christians must distance themselves from sin if they are to remain holy (Romans 6:18). In other words, no life of holiness is possible without righteousness (Romans 6:19). We must keep God's commandments because Jesus said, "If you love me, keep my commandments" (John 14:15).

This list is not exhaustive. However, it perfectly describes the work of the Spirit through the salvation obtained from our Savior Jesus Christ, the salvation by which we have been delivered from slavery and the power of sin once and for all. Sanctification does not imply absolute perfection, but unblemished moral justice demonstrated in purity and obedience and through living righteously.

Distinguishing between different types of sanctification is as crucial as defining the term. In this book, we will discuss 2 types: positional and practical.

Positional sanctification refers to our position in Christ. We are holy because of our position as saved and redeemed in Jesus Christ. The Bible says that we are born again when we give our lives to Jesus. We have been regenerated in Christ, and that is why the Bible labels us as "new creatures." It says in 2 Corinthians 5:17 that "if anyone is in Christ, he is a new creature. Old things have passed away and behold all things have become new." Only Jesus can regenerate us.

Practical sanctification, in turn, implies that Christians are called to constantly fight against the temptation of sin and sin itself. The blood of Jesus indeed saves us, but we must live a life consistent with our position in Jesus. Sanctification is called practical because it concerns everyday life and temptations.

Why a Book on Sanctification?

God has called me into the ministry to accompany His people on the path that leads to Heaven. It is, therefore, my responsibility to push the people of God to constantly live a life of holiness.

This book is a plea, an exhortation inspired by the Lord Jesus, so that sanctification may return to the heart of Christian life. Dear readers, I implore you, by the compassion of Christ, to let the Holy Spirit speak to you as you read this book. I also pray that you let Him lead you towards the life of sanctification that you are called to live until the end of your mission as ambassadors on earth, all the way to the return of Jesus.

The book is divided into four main chapters, covering the following themes:

I- Why a Life of Holiness?

II- The Role of the Holy Spirit in the Life of Sanctification.

III- The Word of God in a Life of Holiness.

IV- (III), The Role of the Shepherd.

Chapter 1:
Why a Life of Holiness?

Christians often reduce sanctification to the mandates to do or not to do. Sanctification is thus summed up as a matter of clothing, a language, a type of association, a way of praying, etc. This is a legalistic conception of sanctification that must be approached carefully. In fact, sanctification is not limited to actions; it starts from the heart.

Living a life of holiness is, first and foremost, a matter of love and obedience to God. Sanctification must not be a heavy burden or an overwhelming load for the disciples of Jesus. Disciples must find in it the only suitable way to live a happy and victorious life in Jesus and with Jesus.

Sanctification is too often misunderstood in the Church, which does not always understand God's will on this subject. Hence, the sanctification of some is based on the fear of a God who is a lawmaker and judge, who is ready to crack down at the first sign of wrongdoing. This is contrary to biblical teaching. It clearly says that "God is slow to anger and rich in kindness" (Psalms 103:8).

For others, sanctification is based on the fear of being judged by others or, worse, the desire to appear better. When it is based on the wrong foundations, sanctification oppresses the disciples of Christ and gradually alienates them from God. This is not God's will for you and me! He wants us to live a life of sanctification so that we may dwell constantly in his presence in perfect communion.

It is, therefore, important to build our life of sanctification on the right foundations. The developments in the first chapter of this reflection on sanctification will, therefore, be devoted to the foundations of sanctification in the lives of disciples of Christ and what they must be built on.

The Holiness of God

God's holiness is the primary foundation for the sanctification of the disciples of Jesus. In Leviticus 19:1-2, the Lord commanded Moses to "speak to the entire assembly of Israel and say to them, 'Be holy because I, the Lord your God, am holy.'"

In Isaiah 6, the prophet describes his experience of God's holiness as follows: "Seraphim stood above him, each with six wings; two with which they covered their faces, two with which they covered their feet, and two with which they flew... They cried Holy, holy, holy is the Lord Almighty."

Holiness is one of God's attributes. However, like love, it is part of what He shares with the new creation to show the world who He is through it. The apostle Peter exhorts us on this subject, saying, "But just as he who called you is holy, so be holy in all you do; for it is written: 'Be holy, because I am holy'" (1 Peter 1:15).

A life of holiness is synonymous with the presence of God in the life of an authentic Christian. It is not a simple presence due to His omnipresence, but a manifest presence revealed to and through the disciples.

Sanctification brings peace and joy because it keeps the disciple in communion with God. The true disciples cannot live without this intimacy. It is the breathing of the spirit and the relaxation of the soul.

At the cross, Jesus paved the way for the restoration of the relationship between God and man that had been broken in Eden. Today, all those who believe in Jesus are called "children of God." However, if the relationship is restored once and for all, communion must nevertheless be maintained by daily efforts to separate ourselves from sin. This principle of separation from sin is fundamental to God's communion with His people.

Separation has two stages, one negative and the other positive. The first is the separation of man morally and spiritually from sin and everything that runs counter to the values of the Kingdom and its justice. The second is closeness to God in an intimate and personal relationship through consecration, worship, and praise. Separation thus leads to a relationship in which God becomes the heavenly Father who lives in us, and we become His sons and daughters.

Each disciple of Christ must encounter moments when the previously stated separations take shape in their stories. No one can escape them and live a worldly and Christian life. There is no connection between the Kingdom of Heaven and the Kingdom of Darkness or between God and Satan.

In the Old Testament, separation was a requirement from which the people of God could not escape under any circumstances. One must "set himself apart" for God or risk provoking His anger. The story of Israel under Assyria's domination is a perfect example (2 Kings 17:6-7). Similarly, the New Testament requires believers to separate themselves from the unhealthy practices of this ungodly world, with a hatred of sin and of everything that does not bring honor to our Lord (John 17:15–16). Therefore, a life of holiness must be a trademark of the Christian because the God we serve is holy.

Sanctification as a Condition for our Salvation

"Seek peace and sanctification, without which no one will see the Lord," says the author of the Epistle to the Hebrews (Hebrews 12:14), where sanctification is presented as a sine qua non condition for salvation. In fact, sanctification is not only a matter of God's will (1 Thessalonians 4:3) but also part of man's new birth, which is also essential for salvation. Jesus said in John 3:3-5 that we cannot see the Kingdom of God unless we are born again.

However, a conflict arises within us between the flesh and the born-again spirit after the new birth. The spirit wants to do God's will, while the flesh constantly wants to bring us back to the instincts of the natural man. It is a battle for holiness that must be won by the Christian in order to be saved.

The Effectiveness of Christian Prayers

Prayer is the best way to talk to God. The Bible exhorts us to pray without ceasing and to make known to God all our needs. All places are suitable for prayer by means of a disposition of the mind. Prayer must be a vital element of the Christian life. In other words, there is no Christian without a life of prayer. Jesus set the example by teaching His disciples to address God in words.

Prayer is not a recipe or a magic formula. The Bible says that we can pray "all kinds of prayers with the Spirit" (Ephesians 6:18). On the other hand, prayer is not a multiplication of empty words. In fact, let's not be like the pagans who keep on babbling, thinking they will be heard because of their many words (Matthew 6:7).

Also, human beings always feel the need to be in communication with the people they love. Therefore, two friends need to talk regularly. That way, they get to know each other more, share good memories, support each other, and trust each other a little more day by day. Our relationship with God becomes steadily more intimate and profound through prayer, in the same way a friendship between two people grows through dialogue. However, a life of prayer is not very effective without a life of holiness.

Sanctification as a Weapon to Fight the "Spirit of Jezebel" in Christian Assemblies

In the Bible, the "spirit of Jezebel" is referred to as a spirit of apostasy, lying, religiosity, manipulation, division, domination, and divorce (Revelation 2:20).

The story of Jezebel is told in 1 Kings 21. She was the wife of Ahab, king of Samaria. There was a man called Naboth who owned a vineyard next to the royal palace. Ahab spoke to Naboth, asking to buy the vineyard. Naboth declined Ahab's offer, arguing that it was an inheritance. Knowing the situation, Jezebel told her husband that she would offer him the vineyard of Naboth of Jezreel. Driven by the spirit of lies, Jezebel then fabricated a story that would lead to the stoning of Naboth, and she eventually took over the land.

A) Fighting the Spirit of Lies

The spirit of lies is still at work today, and its influence is such that lies are trivialized and even applauded at times. Society often labels liars as "clever people."

Lying is the act of uttering words or making statements with the aim of destroying or deceiving while knowing pertinently that they are false. In other words, it is a way of evading the truth by confusing reality or deliberately giving a false impression.

Lying is one of the things that God hates. "There are six things that the Lord hates, seven that are despicable to him: haughty eyes, a lying tongue, hands that shed innocent blood, a heart that devises wicked schemes, feet that are quick to rush into evil, a false witness who pours out lies, and a person who stirs up conflict in the community" (Proverbs 6:16–19). The spirit of lies must have no place in a Christian's heart.

The "spirit of lies" continues to claim victims in our assemblies. When it comes to the truth, some people who call themselves Christians now have the reflex to lie to the point of losing their bearings. Lying becomes an integral part of their lives. The spirit of lies leads even Christians to invent stories with the aim of destroying a brother or a sister.

Some people lie to their spouses, to their employers or employees, to the immigration authorities of a foreign country, about their finances and their social life, just to name a few. For example, a parent who takes the evil pleasure of lying to his or her child is a liar in the same way as what Haitians would call a "professional" liar.

Others push the envelope much further in their imagination, using an inventive wit to embellish their testimony. God does not need a "marketing" team to "sell a story." The believer who bears witness to God's faithfulness does not need to exaggerate or dramatize the facts.

Concerning those who lie, the Bible states in John 8:44 that "you belong to your father, the devil, and you want to carry out your father's desires. He was a murderer from the beginning, not holding to the truth, for there is no truth in him. When he lies, he speaks his native language, for he is a liar and the father of lies."

When it comes to lies, the end does not justify the means because a lie remains what it is, regardless of the reason for which it is told. The Old Testament is filled with examples of lies told by some of God's worthy servants, not to encourage us to follow them but to warn us. Abraham lied and said that Sarah was his sister in order to protect himself against foreign kings who might want to choose his wife as their own. His lie had not spared him. God revealed the truth to the king. His story teaches us to speak the truth, regardless of the consequences.

The biblical verse quoted above emphasizes that anyone who lies continuously is under the influence of the devil. This is not a judgment but rather a logical conclusion based on the Word of God. Additionally, liars have a place that God has reserved for them in Hell, according to Revelations 21:8.

B) Grudge

A grudge is a contained anger with tenacious resentments towards someone because of a wrong or offense endured. It must also be said that grudges are often at the root of slander and lies. Lives are sometimes destroyed with the tongue in a spirit of revenge. This happens even in the Church.

Grudges are the devil's work. If we think all the time about a wrong that was done to us, it reveals a lack of forgiveness and can also lead to a desire for revenge at the opportune moment. The grudge further distances us from the Kingdom of God.

Human relationships are prone to misunderstandings. For this reason, it is important for humans, especially Christians, to cultivate forgiveness. If we do not forget the facts, it simply proves that we have not forgiven because forgiveness implies the definitive forgetting of evil. Furthermore, God has never reminded us of our foolishness.

Love plays a vital role in forgiveness. Psalm 130:3 says that no one could survive if he kept the memory of iniquities. Jesus taught us to pray to God for forgiveness while at the same time forgiving our fellow human beings

(Matthew 6:12). In certain situations, we are encouraged even to give up some of our rights and do without certain things. Jesus urged us not to resist the wicked and to love our enemies, to bless those who curse us, to do good to those who hate us, and to pray for those who mistreat and persecute us (Matthew 5:39, 44).

Furthermore, the tongue can build or destroy, harm others or do good, encourage or discourage. It is said in James 3:10 that "out of the same mouth come praise and cursing. My brothers and sisters, this should not be." In other words, Christians must ensure that their tongue is a source of encouragement with kind words from the Bible, for death and life are at the mercy of the tongue (Proverbs 18:21).

Still, the tongue reveals the believer's relationship with God in the sense that a Christian who is worthy of the name must know that his tongue can corrupt his whole body if the power of God does not tame it (James 3:1–13). Under any circumstances, a saved person cannot spend his time speaking ill of others. We must pray to ask God to take control of our tongue in order to fight any spirit of falsehood or slander (Titus 2:8).

C) Backbiting

Backbiting is a formidable weapon used by Satan, the devil, to destroy our churches in the 21st century. One's words may be true but slanderous at the same time if they are said with the intention of harming others.

In the age of social networking, rumors spread at a dizzying pace. Everyone is quick to share without double-checking. If you are one of those who contribute, in one way or another, to the spread of rumors on social media, you are gossiping! You need to repent because the Bible commands that we speak ill of no one (Titus 3:2).

Most of the time, backbiting conceals other perverse feelings such as jealousy, hatred, and bitterness. Christians must be full of love and refrain from speaking ill of others or spreading rumors that could damage their reputation.

In the past, a servant of God would visit a brother or sister for the sole purpose of praying, praising, or helping. Today, things have changed to the extent that Christians are often gathered to speak ill of their peers. These practices are increasingly present in the hearts of Christians and are opposite to God's will, which is our sanctification. In addition, they can have serious consequences. In Psalms 101:5, God says, "He who secretly slanders his neighbor, I will destroy..." We must be reminded that we serve the God who searches hearts and minds whenever we are tempted by slander.

D) Spirit of Religiosity

All too often, we see pagans who regularly attend church activities (Sunday worship, Bible studies, fasting days, and more) even though they practice a life that is entirely contrary to God's principles and rules.

That is the "religious spirit" at work within churches, ministries, or even with specific individuals.

The story of Jezebel is proof of the different ways in which this spirit manifests itself. Led by this demon, she devised a plan to destroy Naboth. In Ahab's name, she wrote to the inhabitants of Naboth's town, the elders and the magistrates, asking them to publish a fast and to place Naboth at the head of the people so that he could be confronted by two bloodthirsty men whose role was to accuse Naboth of having cursed God and the king in order to have him stoned to death (1 Kings 21:9–12).

Added to this is the story of the prophet Daniel, which is similar to the story of Naboth. Some chiefs and satraps were jealous of Daniel, a servant of God who was endowed with a superior mind, because King Darius was thinking of establishing him over the whole kingdom (Daniel 6:1-3). Unhappy about this situation, they welcomed any opportunity they could find to accuse Daniel.

As a result, they manipulated the king into issuing an irrevocable decree with a stern defense stating, "Anyone who prays to any god or man for a period of thirty days, except to you, will be thrown into the lions' den" (Daniel 6:7-8).In so doing, they knew the outcome in advance. They knew that Daniel would in no way bow down and pray to any god other than the Lord. He would be thrown into the lion's den.

These two biblical accounts show us that the "religious spirit" persecutes God's servants because of their attachment to the Creator. In addition, people led by this spirit loathe the true followers of Jesus. The "religious spirit" is fascinated by gospel songs and appearances instead of focusing on being. These people, who very often put themselves in the ranks of Christians, have an inordinate love for worship, but their hearts remain indifferent to the principles of God.

A religious person is a believer. However, he has no attachment to Jesus. He is only attached to what is done in the ministry. Religious people are constantly in a state of "have you seen me?" because they are not motivated by divine things but rather by trivialities.

We often hear Christians cheering on a worshipper not because the worship blesses them but because they just like the voice, the technique, the stage presence, the outfit, etc. Nonetheless, worship is not just about what is seen. Its effectiveness does not depend solely on the talent of the worshipper, much less on a particular method, for a true worshipper worships in Spirit and truth. This means that the quality of the voice is of no importance if the person from whom the worship comes is not stripped, regenerated, and consecrated.

The Bible tells us that Cain and Abel each decided to make an offering to God. God accepted Abel's offering, while Cain's was rejected because one came from the heart and the other was merely an appearance. If God does not accept the worshipper, He does not accept the offering.

E) Spirit of Manipulation

The "spirit of manipulation" often goes hand in hand with the spirit of lies and is also the source of all kinds of fraud and greed. Regarding this spirit, the Bible says, "No one should wrong or take advantage of a brother or sister. The Lord will punish all those who commit such sins, as we told you and warned you before" (1 Thessalonians 4:6).

The person possessed by this spirit can lead another person into a battle without the latter knowing the ins and outs of it. We often act without reason when dealing with a manipulator. Jezebel manipulated the leaders of the city of Naboth into doing what she wanted.

Today, there are so many manipulators in church that even leaders get involved in the game. Manipulating God's people is a way for them to enrich themselves. They often do so through fund-raising campaigns called by every name in the book (these are not offerings because the Bible is clear about that). They opt for sensational subjects in order to attract the weakest souls. That is why we want to remind you that a Christian's efforts are bound to fail without a life based on sanctification.

F) Spirit of Division

The spirit of Jezebel also refers to a spirit of division. By "spirit of division," I mean a demon who forces a person to sow discord. Sowing discord is something God detests, according to Proverbs 6:19. People who are under the domination of this evil spirit can provoke aversion, mistrust, and division within a group. We are talking about a person who has no restraint. He does not respect the confidentiality of exchanges and goes on to tell what has been secretly confided to him without embarrassment.

As soon as the divisive spirit sits down with another person, its first reaction is to criticize a mutual friend in order to divide them. In other words, it fits comfortably into the pagan maxim of divide and conquer. The person who is possessed by this demon automatically becomes slanderous because it is an effective way of dividing brothers. Nonetheless, the Word of God exhorts us to beware of and keep away from those who cause divisions and scandals to the detriment of the teaching we have received (Romans 16:17).

G) Spirit of Domination

The "spirit of domination" is a demon that pushes some women to reverse roles in the home to the detriment of what the Word of God says. In fact, the Scriptures urge us "to realize that the head of every man is Christ, and the head of the woman is man, and the head of Christ is God" (1 Corinthians 11:3). Based on this logic, it is up to the man to take charge of the family.

Conversely, we are witnessing the emergence of a worldly movement adopted by certain church leaders, promoting the woman as head of the family with the intention of dominating the husband. This movement, called "feminism," is the work of the devil because it seeks to destroy the family. By reversing the functions, the wife must no longer be submissive to her husband. Yet the woman was not created to dominate but to be dominated in an environment saturated with love and respect from her husband. As a result, the wife must indeed be submissive, but her husband must also love her. If Adam was created before Eve, it was because God wanted man to be the head of the family.

Today, there is a tendency to put men and women in competition with each other, whereas they should each fulfill their functions as described by the Word of God. Husband and wife are not equal because they do not fulfill the same functions. Regardless of the social and economic differences between men and women, the man remains the head of the family, and that has nothing to do with the masculinity that some feminists talk about. Whether you are a nurse or a doctor, your husband is your boss, even if he is a shoe shiner. Otherwise, it is an abomination.

Jezebel was ridden by this "spirit of domination" that causes women to question the family hierarchy established by God. That spirit of domination can be manifested by excessive control of the husband's income to prevent him from helping anyone else. Such a desire to control everything fits in perfectly with the logic of Jezebel's spirit in view of the influence she exerts over Ahab.

It must be pointed out, however, that the husband, as head of the family, has obligations. He must work to take care of his family. Nowadays, some husbands spend most of their time caring for trivial things instead of taking an interest in their family on the pretext that the wife has sufficient means to meet the family's needs. If you are not sick and you meet all the conditions to find a job but would rather leave the function of caring for the family solely to your wife, know that you are not a good husband in God's eyes because "anyone who does not provide for their relatives, and especially for their own household, has denied the faith and is worse than an unbeliever" (1 Timothy 5:8).

H) The Fight Against Demons Opposing Marriage

Marriage is the first institution created by God when he united Adam and Eve. Satan has never liked marriage. He has been fighting it ever since Eden. Today, the institution is weakened. Many people refuse to marry, others marry for the wrong reasons, and finally, many marriages end in divorce.

This proves that the devil has not given up. Young couples tend to claim victory after marriage, whereas the survival of a marriage over time requires much more prayer and perseverance than marriage itself. Sometimes, a man and a woman who have been living together in perfect harmony decide to get married. After the wedding, all the problems arise, and they divorce.

You should know that a bad marriage can prevent the salvation of a Christian if the life that exists within that marriage is not in conformity with God's will. However, God hates repudiation (divorce) (Malachi 2:16). Divorces are sometimes a source of hatred, revenge, and other practices that are considered abominations in God's eyes.

On the other hand, some separations are necessary if the rules of separation are respected. A husband who violates his wife verbally, psychologically, or physically is not fulfilling his role because the Bible says that he must love his wife. The Bible says, "To the married I give this command (not I, but the Lord): A wife must not separate from her husband. But if she does, she must remain unmarried or else be reconciled to her husband. And a husband must not divorce his wife" (1 Corinthians 7:10). However, an exception to this principle is made in the 11th verse on the condition that the woman remains unmarried or is reconciled to her husband. Otherwise, it is a flagrant case of adultery according to the Word of God (we will address this in the second chapter in the section on the sanctification of the body).

Christians need to understand that demons lurk around marriage. Prayer must, therefore, be at the heart of marriage, both for those considering it and for those who have already entered it.

Repentance

One of the purposes of preaching the gospel is to bring the sinner to awareness of his state in order to turn to God. In His mercy, God always allows time for the person who lives a life contrary to his principles to change and return to the path of holiness. This is why 2 Peter 3:9 teaches us that the Lord does not delay in fulfilling the promise, as some think, but is patient with you, not wanting any to sin but wanting all to come to repentance. The Bible says, "When you are in distress and all these things have happened to you, then in later days you will return to the Lord your God and obey him" (Deuteronomy 4:30). Thus, God always expects us to be converted at some point. This process of conversion is known as "repentance."

Repentance is the feeling of regret for one's sins. It is a step towards conversion. Repentance is always followed by a feeling of regret (sadness), which is at the root of conversion. Apostle Paul tells us in 2 Corinthians 7:10 that sadness, according to God, necessarily produces a repentance to salvation from which we never repent, whereas the sadness of the world produces death.

This awareness of the sinner's situation is the work of the power of the living God, who searches hearts and minds. As such, God grants repentance to the Gentiles so that they may have life (Acts 11:18).

On the other hand, the fruits of repentance are manifest in the sense that it is not enough to pronounce the Word, but there is conduct related to it. This is why the Word of God commands us to produce fruits worthy of repentance (Matthew 3:8). In other words, a Christian does not have to present himself to be recognized as such. He must simply live it.

In addition, repentance is compulsory for those who want to enter the Kingdom of God because Jesus said, "Repent, for the kingdom of heaven is near" (Matthew 4:17). It is also a miracle of God when we feel uncomfortable in the presence of sin and abstain from it as a result. Based on the Bible, we can affirm that repentance is one of the first impacts of God's Word.

We recall the day of Pentecost, when the disciples of Jesus were all filled with the Holy Spirit (Acts 2:4). One of the words spoken by Peter on behalf of the disciples was, "Repent and let every one of you be baptized in the name of Jesus Christ for the forgiveness of your sins, and you will receive the gift of the Holy Spirit" (Acts 2:38). Verse 40 of the same book and chapter states that about three thousand people accepted Jesus as their Lord and Savior as a result. This implies that repentance is synonymous with conversion and must necessarily lead to a life of holiness.

However, remorse is not enough to speak of repentance. Judah was remorseful, and this was undoubtedly the cause of his suicide, but he had not repented. Though, his fate would have been completely different if he had asked God for forgiveness. This lack of repentance definitively condemned him to Hell.

God uses His children to spread the message of repentance. He expects us to conform to His rules. If we persist in evil practices, we will be struck by his wrath. The Church at Thyatira was warned because of His leniency toward sin. The Bible says that God threatened to send great tribulation to this group of sinners in Thyatira if they did not repent of their deeds (Revelation 2:22). God again showed His mercy by giving these sinners time to repent.

Chapter 2:
The Role of the Holy Spirit in the Life of Sanctification

Now that we have laid the foundations of sanctification, we can begin to think about the "how." I know I must live a life of sanctification, but how do I go about it?

I said it at the beginning of the first chapter. Sanctification is not simply a matter of rituals or of observing principles. It comes from our relationship with God. Hence, I must tell you about the person who makes it possible for us to live this life of sanctification before giving you some important keys to living a practical life of holiness: The Holy Spirit!

Who is the Holy Spirit?

At first glance, we must recognize the Holy Spirit's involvement in creation. The Bible says that the Spirit of God moved over the waters, referring to the presence of the Holy Spirit (Genesis 1:2). In the Old Testament, the Holy Spirit was primarily the channel through which prophets received messages and spoke for God (2 Samuel 23:2).

In its turn, the New Testament tells us that the Holy Spirit is "in you" and "with you" (John 14:17). It also states that the Holy Spirit dwells in us permanently (1 Corinthians 6:19) in the sense that he is a power that we have received (Acts 1:8) and which enables us to walk by the Spirit (Romans 8:4-6).

The Holy Spirit is God. He is the third person of the Trinity, the arm through which God moves and acts in our lives. The Bible teaches that He has a Spirit (Romans 8:27), a will (1 Corinthians 12:11), and emotions (Ephesians 4:30).

The Holy Spirit is God, like the Father and the Son. They are on an equal footing because they have a person-to-person relationship with each other. "Go and make disciples of all nations, baptizing them in the name of the Father and of the Son and of the Holy Spirit" (Matthew 28:19). This Bible verse proves that the Holy Spirit is on the same level as the Father and the Son.

Moreover, the Bible says that the Holy Spirit is also a comforter in the same way as Jesus (John 14:16–17), and the grace of the Son, the love of the Father, and the fellowship of the Holy Spirit are elevated to the same rank (2 Corinthians 13:14). Holiness is unique to God. And the Spirit is depicted as "Holy." Thus, there is no doubt that it is the Spirit of God, for only God is holy (Acts 5:3–4), and when the Holy Spirit speaks, it is God who speaks (Hebrews 10:15–17).

Added to this are the titles given to the Holy Spirit, which, once again, leave no doubt that He is God. We find the following designations:

- Spirit of the Living God (2 Corinthians 3:3).
- Spirit of Christ (Romans 8:9).
- Spirit of the Lord (Luke 4:18).
- Spirit of your Father (Matthew 10:20).
- Spirit of holiness (Romans 1:4).
- Spirit of Jesus (Acts 16:7).

The Holy Scriptures also has other characteristics belonging exclusively to God, which are also attributed to the Holy Spirit, such as truth (John 14:16-17), omniscience (1 Corinthians 2:10-11), life (John 6: 63), omnipresence (Psalms 139:7), eternity (Hebrews 9:14), omnipotence (Romans 8:11), and love (Romans 5:5).

The Holy Spirit is the comforter (paraclete in the New Testament) in the sense that Jesus himself said that the Father would send the Holy Spirit in His name to teach us exhaustively and to remind us of everything He has said to us (John 14:26). In other words, he is there to help Christians.

In a very special way, the Holy Spirit was sent by the Father and the Son into the world on the day of Pentecost to: (1) make the work of the church much more effective; (2) baptize believers so that they can bear witness and produce fruits of the Spirit; and (3) to convince sinners once and for all. In other words, the ministry of the Holy Spirit is to continue the work that Jesus Christ began when He walked the earth, which consists of convincing those who do not believe in God, who risk losing their souls, and who need salvation.

The Holy Spirit is necessary for the Church in general and for Christians in particular. As far as believers are concerned, the Holy Spirit gives them a spirit of discernment that enables them to recognize false spirits and doctrines and, at the same time, makes it easier to distinguish truth from lies (1 John 4:1–4). He can direct, control, influence, and lead the believers who are subject to Him (Ephesians 5:18; Romans 8:14). The Holy Spirit makes it easier to understand and accept the things of God (1 Corinthians 2:10–15, 1 John 2:20–27). He helps believers in their moments of weakness (Romans 8:26–27, Ephesians 6:18) and promotes the production of fruits of the Spirit in Christian lives with the aim of resembling Christ (Galatians 5:16–22–25).

The Holy Spirit also actively participates in the purification process of the Christian from sin (Romans 2:29). His presence forces the Christian to sanctify Himself (Romans 15:16). The Holy Spirit regenerates (Titus 3:5) and ensures the believer's salvation (Romans 8:16).

No Christian can please God without the Holy Spirit. The presence of the Holy Spirit makes the Christian a special person endowed with power that differentiates him from the pagan. We are all God's creatures, but we are different. It is impossible to imagine a Christian without the power of God, which is the fruit of the Holy Spirit.

God's people are recognized through His power. We do not have to be afraid of anyone because we are covered by this power that makes us brave. This power, born of the Spirit of holiness, has no rival. When Moses and Aaron gave the message that God had sent to Pharaoh, he made them perform a miracle by turning the rod into a snake. Pharaoh called in his magicians, who did the same. The Bible says that Aaron's rod swallowed up those of Pharaoh's magicians (Exodus 7:10–12). This is the same power that the Holy Spirit gives us because God does not change and is the same yesterday, today, and forever, says the Word of God.

A doctor friend of mine was targeted by some voodoo practitioners in the countryside of Haiti, where he worked. One day, he decided to hand his life over to Jesus for protection. The criminals, who formed a group (known in Haiti as "bann chanprèl"), informed him that he had no escape from their grip. While my friend was in a night fasting service, the Holy Spirit intervened through a servant of God, declaring to him that he was protected by the power of the Holy Spirit, notwithstanding the diabolical ceremony ordered at the time to destroy him. We are permanently protected when we live a life of holiness.

There is no evangelist, no preacher, no pastor, and no bishop without the power of the Holy Spirit. Apostle Paul spoke to the Christians of Corinth, mentioning his state of weakness and fear (1 Corinthians 2:3). However, he made it clear that his words and preaching were not based on convincing speeches of mere wisdom but on proof of the Spirit and power as the foundation of faith (1 Corinthians 2:4–5). This is why Jesus urged the disciples to stay in Jerusalem until they were clothed with power from above before preaching repentance and forgiveness (Luke 24:49).

We are not ordinary people in the eyes of the pagans, thanks to the power generated by the Holy Spirit. And Jesus showed this power constantly during the 33 years He lived on earth. He defied the laws of physics by walking on water and raised Lazarus from the dead after 4 days. We must imitate Jesus, who was not ordinary.

When God asked Moses to return to Egypt to tell Pharaoh to free His people, the Bible says that the

Lord made Moses a god for Pharaoh (Exodus 7:1). This passage from the Bible is proof that God delegated His authority to us in order to make His power known to the unbelievers. Nevertheless, we must cultivate a life that is conducive to the demands of the Holy Spirit.

I remember a day when I took the elevator in a place where I was participating in an event. When I walked out, the other person who was riding along with me asked, "Who are you?" Without answering the question, I asked him to explain his problem because he had been staring at me since I entered the elevator. He replied that he noticed a light shining on my forehead. I revealed to him that I was a man of God. He went all over the hotel, telling people how he had just met a man of God. This testimony proves that even pagans can recognize the power that is within us.

Nowadays, many Christian assemblies do not experience the power and anointing of the Holy Spirit. That is because He does not dwell where we refuse to do God's will. This lack of power makes us seem ordinary when, in fact, we are not, thanks to our position in Christ. COVID-19 causing the doors of sanctuaries to be shut is proof of this. We suffered in the same way as the pagans, who were supposed to find refuge in the Church.

We must remember the pool at Bethesda, where an angel of God came down from time to time to stir the water. The Holy Scriptures mention the healing of the person who went down there first after the water had been agitated, regardless of his illness (John 5:2-4). This biblical account shows that the power of the Holy Spirit casts out demons and heals all diseases. The Church is still missing that power. We are not spared from the plagues that attack the world because of our inability to live a holy life so that the Holy Spirit can resonate within us. Yet the Bible says that our God commands us to be mighty (Psalms 68:28). The Spirit of God is ready to manifest its presence in us and around us on the sole condition that we live a life of holiness.

The Church is called to make a difference in this ungodly world because Jesus tells us that we are Peter (in the sense of worthy preachers of the Word of Christ). Upon this rock, He will build His church, and the gates of Hell shall not prevail against it (Matthew 16:18). We are so unique that we are called a chosen race, a royal priesthood, a holy nation, and a people of His possession (1 Peter 2:9).

Therefore, we can affirm that a Christian is synonymous with power, according to the Bible. We are talking about the real power that allows us to dominate over satanic forces, to lay hands on the sick, and to work miracles in the name of Jesus.

I was on a mission in a very remote area of Haiti. The old house that welcomed me had only a curtain that served as a door at the entrance. There was a demonic spirit causing the drowning of many children in the area. The Lord ordered me to go and rout out this evil spirit. I effectively commanded this demon to be thrown into the abyss in the powerful name of Jesus.

That evening, no one else was at home, but Jesus was with me. I woke up when it was barely midnight to find a group of people who were unhappy with the situation surrounding the house at the instigation of that spirit. I prostrated myself to pray to God, asking him to intervene on my behalf. Before long, I saw a lightning bolt landing at the entrance to the house, appearing to barricade it. I assure you, brothers and sisters, the mob was dispersed, and I was able to rest all night without noticing anything more.

That day, I experienced the power of the Holy Spirit. This power depends on our relationship with God. It exists in fasting, in prayer, and in living a life focused on the works of the Spirit.

Speaking in Tongues

Many people believe that "speaking in tongues" is evidence of the Holy Spirit. I contest this assertion because Jesus never spoke in tongues during his time on earth, although He always showed evidence of the Holy Spirit in Him. "Speaking in tongues" is a manifestation of the Holy Spirit, not the evidence of the Holy Spirit. As for the evidence of the Holy Spirit in someone's life, the apostle Paul refers us to the fruits of the Spirit.

The Works of the Spirit

Flesh and blood alone cannot faithfully serve God without the help of the Spirit. Moreover, the battle we are waging is not carnal but instead spiritual. Any attempt to fight sin with the flesh alone is doomed to failure. Apostle Paul tells us that we don't do the good we want to do, and we do the evil we do not want because the flesh tends to get the better of us (Romans 7:19–20). Hence, the importance of the works of the Spirit.

We have been baptized and made to drink by the Spirit into the body of Christ (1 Corinthians 12:13). We have also been regenerated by Him, who transformed us so that we may be clothed with a new nature. By agreeing to be guided by the Spirit, we are children of God, who has adopted us through the Spirit (Romans 8:14–16).

As a result, we do not have to live according to the flesh because the Spirit of Christ has resided in us. In other words, Christ is formed in us and lives in us (Galatians 4:19; Colossians 1:27); the feelings of Christ work in us to conform us to His image (1 Philippians 2:5; Romans 8:29). This means that the life of holiness we must live lies in the personality and will of Christ if we surrender to Him.

The Bible says that we are clearly an open letter from Christ, written not with ink but with the Spirit of the living God on our hearts (2 Corinthians 3:2–3). This verse refers to the personality of Christ that must shine in us.

We must be like Him by following His example when He was on earth because He never sinned. We have crucified the flesh, and we must produce the fruits of the Spirit (Galatians 5:23), which are:

- Love, one of the first sentiments that we inherited from Jesus. As His disciples, we must love one another because God is love, and whoever loves is born of God and knows God, whereas anyone who does not love does not know God (1 John 4:7-8). We must also love those who do not love us. A loving heart has no room for jealousy and other practices that are not in accordance with God's will (1 Corinthians 13:4–5).

- Joy, the work of the Holy Spirit (Romans 14:17). This joy is independent of the modifications of life and any trial because the joy of the Lord is our strength (Nehemiah 8:10) and our names are written in Heaven (Luke 10:20). The world cannot give us the joy that we find in abundance in Jesus (Psalms 16:11). Christians must turn trials into a cause for joy by giving glory to God (James 1:2).

- Peace, issued from the character of God, who Himself always gives it to His children in all ways (2 Thessalonians 3:16). We have inherited it from Jesus (John 16:33), who gives it to us so that our hearts may not be troubled (John 14:27). This means that Jesus has given us an inner peace that leads us to have peace with our neighbors and to cultivate it even when we are disturbed (Matthew 5:9).

- Patience, a weapon that enables us to see the fulfillment of God's promises (Hebrews 10:36) and save our souls (Luke 21:19). God is always patient with us so that we may repent of our sins (2 Peter 3:9).

- Kindness, indicating politeness and friendliness. God wants us to be kind to everyone (2 Timothy 2:24).

- Compassion, synonymous with gentleness. The Bible commands us to be gentle in our responses so as not to provoke anger in others (Proverbs 15:1).

- Faithfulness, which we must practice in our relationships (faithfulness in marriage will be addressed in the section on sanctification of the body).

- Gentleness, meaning not being prone to anger. The Bible specifies that gentleness should be known to all (Philippians 4:5). In other words, we must be gentle with everyone. Gentleness requires us to show moderation and humility in our dealings with others. Additionally, Jesus taught us to be gentle when He was on earth (Matthew 11:29).

- Temperance, for its part, demands self-control. It is about showing wisdom while holding back all passion (Proverbs 29:11). Temperance requires discipline, moderation, and restraint.

In short, the works of the Spirit are the evidence of the Holy Spirit in the life of the believer, while "speaking tongues" is a manifestation of the Holy Spirit.

Baptism

Baptism is one of the two ordinances available to Christians. It is a conscious commitment. This means that minors and the mentally ill cannot be baptized. There are 2 types of baptism: baptism by sprinkling, performed mainly by Catholics, and baptism by immersion, supported by Protestants. The first involves pouring a few drops of water over the head of the person being baptized. The second involves dipping the person being baptized in water.

For us Protestant Christians, "to baptize" means to plunge. Total immersion symbolizes death to sin, and coming out of the water symbolizes resurrection with Christ. The Bible specifies that, having been buried with Him in baptism, we have also been resurrected in him and with Him through faith in the power of God, who raised Him from the dead (Colossians 2:12).

In addition, Jesus was baptized by immersion (Matthew 3:16). Despite the importance of baptism for Christians, it does not save. "Whoever believes and is baptized will be saved, but whoever does not believe will be condemned" (Mark 16:16). Given this biblical account, it is not baptism that saves us, but our belief, our faith in Jesus. It is true that we receive the Holy Spirit from the moment we accept Jesus as Lord and Savior. However, the Bible indicates that the Spirit of God descended on Jesus after He came out of the water (Matthew 3:16).

The Holy Communion

The Holy Communion is the second ordinance in which the baptized, commonly called members of the Church, take the bread that symbolizes the body of Jesus and the wine that reminds us of his blood. In other words, it is the Lord's Supper.

We must eat the bread and drink the cup with dignity. If we do not, we are guilty of sinning against the blood and body of Christ (1 Corinthians 11:27). We must also check ourselves, meaning it is up to us to assess whether we are fit to take the Lord's Supper (1 Corinthians 11:28). It is by producing the works of the Spirit that we can ascertain whether we are worthy to partake in Christ's meal. If we fail to respect these principles, we may be struck with illness (1 Corinthians 11:30). Consequently, being baptized is not enough to partake in the Lord's Supper, but a life of holiness is necessary.

Sanctification of the Body

In recent years, several preachers of diabolical permissiveness have been promoting a liberal conception of the Word of God. Contrary to the Bible, they establish a hierarchy between body, soul, and spirit. In the opinion of these men and women, the body is of no importance to God. I am against this way of thinking because the Bible says, "May God himself, the God of peace, sanctify you through and through. May your whole spirit, soul and body be kept blameless at the coming of our Lord Jesus Christ" (1 Thessalonians 5:23).

Considering this verse, the body is of the same value as the soul and the spirit in the eyes of God, whether you are on the side of the trichotomy or the dichotomy. Plus, we must glorify God in our bodies and our spirits because they belong to God, as written in 1 Corinthians 6:20.

We sing all the time that our bodies, our hearts, and our souls no longer belong to us because God's love claims them, while we refuse to respect the rules of conduct relating to the sanctification of the body. In fact, Apostle Paul tells us that we are God's temple, and therefore God's Spirit dwells in us (1 Corinthians 3:16). This means that our bodies are the temple of the Holy Spirit, who cannot dwell in a body that has not been set apart for God. Hence, the importance of sanctifying the body.

Sanctified Eyes

What we see influences what we think. This means that most of the things we remember pass through our eyes. In this sense, the Bible states that the eye is the lamp that illuminates the body if it is in good condition, and if this part of the body is not in good condition, the body, in general, will wander in darkness (Matthew 6:22–23).

The eye is one of the most chosen sensory receptors for receiving information. It is a gateway to the heart and soul. We must refrain from placing evil things before our eyes so that our spirits can remain intact (Psalms 101: 3). That is why David asked God to spare his eyes from all vanities (Psalms 119: 37).

Temptation is the first step toward sin (James 1:14–15). Satan tempted Jesus, but He never sinned. The Bible says that the devil took Him to a mountain so that He could have a panoramic view of the kingdoms of the world. Satan told Him that he could give him all these things if He bowed down and worshipped him. Jesus chased him off the mountain, declaring that only God should be worshipped (Matthew 4:8–10).

The example of Jesus reveals a truth: Satan knows that our minds are easily affected by our eyes. Thus, we need to keep our eyes away from temptation. A Christian, for example, cannot watch just any movie or subscribe to just any social networking page so as not to expose himself to temptation.

Nevertheless, some situations are beyond our control. Nowadays, it is hard to differentiate between some people who claim to be believers and those who are pagan because they dress the same way. This can sometimes cause temptation. If so, look away so as not to extend the temptation because it can also lead to lust.

Ultimately, we must abstain from the temptations of the eyes because Jesus taught us that the eyes are closely related to the body. Therefore, to achieve a healthy body, we must sanctify our eyes.

Clothing

Several biblical accounts prove that bad clothing is not pleasing to God. Many people say that appearance is not important. Yet the Bible says, "I also want the women to dress modestly, with decency and propriety, adorning themselves, not with elaborate hairstyles or gold or pearls or expensive clothes" (1 Timothy 2:9). When God asked Jacob to go to Bethel, he asked his household and all the people with him to separate themselves from foreign gods, to sanctify themselves, and to change their clothes (Genesis 35:1–2).

Jacob demanded that they change their clothes because he knew full well that some of the clothes did not please God. The Bible says that they gave Jacob all the foreign gods, including the rings they wore (Genesis 35:4). From this verse, we deduce that a servant of God, worthy of the name, cannot wear rings and other related jewelry. Christians must necessarily show modesty in outward dress in general and clothing in particular.

The Bible tells us that people who refuse to dress chastely are acting under the impulse of demons. The Holy Scriptures tell us the story of the man from Gadara who constantly took off his clothes because a demon possessed him. Jesus cast out the demon, and the man no longer had this attitude once he had regained all his cognitive abilities (Luke 8:27–35).

The sanctification of the body requires Christians not to wear just any clothes. A woman must refrain from wearing clothes that reveal her shape, as if she were half naked. Besides, God, in His holiness, even places fruits in their wrappings so that they are not naked. This means that the body must be decently covered because it is of great importance in a life of holiness.

Concerning the distinction made by the Word of God between a man's clothing and that of a woman (Deuteronomy 22:5), world society, including certain leaders, plunges into terrible hypocrisy. It is normal, in their view, for a woman to wear a pair of pants and a shirt. Conversely, a man who wears a skirt and a blouse will be mocked. It's true that the word "pants" is not mentioned in the verse, but pants remain a man's clothing, and therefore, according to the Bible, a woman should not wear them. These practices taint the body, which is the temple of the Holy Spirit.

Tattoos

In addition to the clothing matter, other practices such as tattoos, fake nails, and wigs can taint our bodies. God warns us not to make incisions in our flesh and not to print on us (Leviticus 19:28). According to the Bible, we should detest any form of imprinting on the flesh.

Make-up

Make-up is linked to vanity. It is a practice contrary to God's will, which is our separation from the world. I'm not saying that a servant of God should not look good. However, it must be done with modesty. Let us recall the story of Esther, who, unlike the other potential brides, did not wear make-up to present herself before the king (Esther 2:13–15).

Eyelid make-up (eyelash extensions, eye shadows, wigs, and other practices) first appeared in ancient Egypt around 3000 B.C. Corrupt women and prostitutes introduced it with the aim of creating sex appeal. This practice is mentioned in Proverbs 6:25, which states, "Do not lust in your heart after her beauty or let her captivate you with her eyes." The Bible also says that Jezebel, Ahab's wife, put on make-up to seduce Jehu, Israel's anointed king, who had the task of destroying Ahab's family (2 Kings 9:30).

In view of the above, we can see that God disapproves of this practice and invites Christians to take care of themselves with decency and modesty.

Fornication

Fornication refers to all unlawful sexual practices and relationships. The Bible tells us that we must abstain from fornication (Acts 15:14). It refers to sexual relations outside the bonds of marriage, sexual lovemaking outside marriage, male and female masturbation, pornography, homosexuality, incest, and all other related practices such as the use of sex toys, abortions, sexual relations with animals, and fantasizing about having sex with another person who is not one's spouse.

Sex outside of marriage violates the sacred character of marriage and sex, which are meant for procreation. Sometimes, sex outside of marriage can lead to consequences such as unwanted pregnancies and even sexually transmitted diseases. Paul told the Christians of Corinth that there was fornication among them, which was not found even among the pagans (1 Corinthians 5:1). Fornication makes the Holy Spirit sad. The Word of God exhorts us to flee from fornication, for whoever fornicates sins against his own body (1 Corinthians 6:18). A young girl once called me after a service to say that she was missing my voice. I told her to go find one of the electronic platforms and listen to my sermons so that she could satisfy her craving. The Holy Spirit within me enabled me to escape the immoral intentions of this young girl.

Adultery

Adultery is committed when a married man or woman has sex with another person. It is one of the sins of the flesh (Matthew 15:19–20).

The author of the Epistle to the Hebrews refers to this exhortation, stating: "Marriage should be honored by all, and the marriage bed kept pure, for God will judge the adulterer and all the sexually immoral" (Hebrews 13:4).

Still, the apostle Paul describes another form of adultery. It is true that God hates divorce, but certain situations require it. Nevertheless, if you must separate, you shall not enter a relationship with any other person as long as your spouse is alive. Otherwise, this is considered adultery (Romans 7:2–3; 1 Corinthians 7:10–11).

Chapter 3:
The Word of God
in a Life of Holiness

In the Holy Scriptures, the expression "Word of God" refers, on the one hand, to the messages of God (*rema*) (Luke 11:28).

In this sense, the Word of God is His spokesperson. Yet, it seems like the title "Word of God" applies to someone whom God uses to communicate information and instructions. Jesus tells us that everything he says comes from God, and He says it as the Father told Him (John 12:49–50). On the other hand, it refers to the Bible (logos) as the compass for Christians (2 Timothy 3:16).

The Bible is the Word of God given to all men, all nations, all races, and all cultures. It is the inspired Word of God, but it is not outside our reality. The Word of God transcends time and surpasses human intelligence. It is a sacred book in which we find answers about the purpose and meaning of life, about education, family, forgiveness, and the life of holiness.

The Word of God preceded all creatures because the Bible says that in the beginning was the Word, and the Word was with God, and the Word was God (John 1:1).

Verse 3 of the same chapter asserts that "through him all things were made; without him nothing was made that has been made."

It is, therefore, important to consider the role of the Bible (the Word of God) in the process of Christian sanctification.

1. Putting God's Word into Practice

We must put the Word of God into practice, knowing that the Bible is not an ordinary book, much less a collection of old manuscripts full of lies. In fact, one of the characteristics of the Word of God is that it is true, because the Bible tells us that truth is the foundation of the Word of God (Psalms 119:160).

We must establish a substantial difference between facts and truth. The truth found in God's Word is more than just a fact. A person who allows God's Word to shape his or her thoughts and activities gains a spiritual and life-giving understanding of truth. However, we must take several steps before meeting the conditions to put it into practice.

The first step in putting God's Word into practice is to read it. Having a Bible does not make you a Christian because also pagans have them. It must be read and acknowledged as the Word of God. A Christian worthy of the name must read the Bible daily. In doing so, we set for ourselves the goal of learning to know God and His will for us. When we read the Bible, we discover a succession of reassuring elements, such as God's plan for our redemption, His promises, and His character. We also gain insight into the life of holiness. Additionally, this knowledge of God that we gain from the Holy Scriptures provides a solid foundation for putting the principles of the Bible into practice in our Christian lives.

The second step is to study the Bible. Clearly, to study a book, you must be able to read it, but reading is not enough. God is the true author of the Bible. Therefore, the best way to study the Word of God is to pray that the author (God) Himself will help us to understand a theme, a subject, or any book in the Bible and to produce coherent reflections on them while considering the context because the Bible does not contradict itself.

The third stage calls for "memorizing" the Word of God. Memorizing the Word of the Lord does not mean simply mobilizing cognitive processes, even though it is impossible to put into practice what we do not remember. Indeed, the psalmist David said, "I will hold your word in my heart, that I may not sin against you" (Psalm

119:11). This Scripture means that we must first memorize the Word of Christ before even thinking of holding it in our hearts. By memorizing God's Word, we move towards sanctification as we keep sin far from us.

The fourth step is to "meditate" on God's Word. Meditating on God's Word is one of the greatest keys that open the paths to understanding and truth. To meditate is to fill our thoughts with the thoughts of God. In other words, meditating on the Word leads us to surrender ourselves to God while contemplating the promises He has made. We become absorbed in what God has said. Thus, it becomes easier for us to do His will.

Added to this is the knowledge that comes from meditating on God's Word. It is mentioned in Psalms 119:130 that "The revelation of your words enlightens; it gives understanding to the simple." Reading the Word of God without meditating on it is like eating without digesting.

Jesus also showed us this through the parable of the sower. In this case, a sower went out to sow (Matthew 13:4). Some of the seed fell into stony places where there was not much soil, and it was burned and withered away because it did not find deep soil, although it sprang up immediately (Matthew 13:5–6). This part of the seed refers to someone who has heard and received the Word but does not let it take root within (Matthew 13:20–21). These verses reveal the importance of meditating on the Word of God.

It is worth knowing that meditation not only multiplies our knowledge but also helps us to understand God and His Word better. When we begin to meditate on the Word of God, we are enlightened by understanding the conduct that God expects of us. One of the aims of meditation is to put us in a position to practice God's Word. Meditation "day and night" will lead us to respect everything that is said in the Holy Scriptures. The Word and the knowledge of revelation will enable us to act according to the Lord's will. We become more productive as the Word of God takes up space in our lives.

God wants us to be models for the world. In other words, He wants us to be an open book for all the people around us. Just as Jesus was the reflection of His glory and the imprint of His person (Hebrews 1:3), we must be like Him. To do this, we must give ourselves completely to what God has said. We must become totally absorbed in His commandments. When we give ourselves totally to meditating on God's Word, He becomes actively involved in our lives. Knowing that He is a God of justice and mercy, He commits himself to us if we devote ourselves to His Word.

The Bible tells us to meditate on God's Word day and night (Joshua 1:8; Psalms 1:1–3). This does not mean spending 24 hours doing nothing but reading the Bible, especially as meditation is not just reading.

Nevertheless, the Word of God must not always be far from our lips. In this regard, Paul tells us that the

Word is close to us, in our mouths and in our hearts (Romans 8:10). God's Word is full of power, and we need that power to produce fruit in us.

It is very easy to meditate anytime and anywhere. Psalm 63:6 tells us: "When I think of you on my bed, I meditate on you during the watches of the night." As soon as we remember the character and greatness of God, we are in full meditation on God and His Word. Meditation makes our minds and emotions more secure. It is a potent tool that we can use to keep our minds under control. The flesh cannot take precedence over our spirit when we meditate on the Word of God and acquire the renewed mind of Christ.

Thus, we feed on the Word of the Lord, allowing its power and the revelation of God's promises to come true in us, for man does not live by bread alone but by every word that proceeds out of the mouth of God (Matthew 4:4). The person who lives in perfect harmony with the Word of God constantly rectifies his state of mind and even his way of life.

Ultimately, we must remember that the life of sanctification requires us to put the Word of God into practice in order to sharpen our discernment and help us to better distinguish between good and evil (Hebrews 5:14). That is why it is essential to study, memorize, and meditate on the Word of God to put it into practice. However, we need to be reassured that we are not alone in our efforts to put the Lord's Word into practice. We have the Holy Spirit dwelling within us (John 14:17).

Therefore, we can only know our Savior, Jesus Christ, through the Holy Spirit. We can only know the Holy Spirit through the Word of God because He teaches nothing that is contrary to the Word.

2. The Benefits of the Word of God

It is true that the Bible remains the best-selling and most translated book in the world. Yet very little is said about the benefits of the Word of God. In this section, we are going to take stock of the matter.

2.1. The Word of God Creates Faith in Us

To speak of faith is to first say that it is saving (Ephesians 2:8). The Holy Scriptures define faith as a firm assurance of things hoped for, a demonstration of things not seen (Hebrews 11:1). The story of Rahab is a perfect example of this faith. The prostitute, who was to become an ancestor of Jesus, hid 2 spies from Israel on the roof of her house. She showed her faith in God by telling the spies that all the inhabitants trembled before them because they had the Lord in their camp (Joshua 2:4–10). This statement is enough to speak of Rahab's faith.

However, faith without good deeds is dead (James 2:26). Our faith in Jesus must be based on the Word. The Bible tells us that "faith comes from hearing, and hearing comes from the Word of Christ." This means that faith in the Word of God precedes our salvation. It is by faith that we recognize that the Word of God created the world and that the invisible creates the visible (Hebrews 11:3).

The same applies to the life of holiness, which also requires faith in the Word, because without faith, it is impossible to please God (Hebrews 11:6). We do not practice adultery because we believe that it is contrary to the will of the Lord. It is also the Word that tells us how to behave in order to inherit the Kingdom of God. Faith does not simply mean believing in miracles. We also fight sin by faith, which is the first of the benefits that the Word of God gives us and which is the "...shield with which we can extinguish all the fiery darts of the evil one" (Ephesians 6:16).

2.2. The Power of the Word

When we study the Bible and absorb it, all the creative power of God's Word is at work in us because God used nothing other than His Word and His Spirit to create the universe. This same power of the Word is transmitted to us in the Bible. Paul told the Christians in Thessalonica that we give thanks to God continually because, when they heard the Word of God, they received it, not as the word of men but as the Word of God working in us who are believers (1 Thessalonians 2:13).

The Word of God is like rain and snow descending from Heaven to water, fertilize the earth, and make the plants blossom, because it does not return to God without effect, without having carried out His will and fulfill His purposes (Isaiah 55:10–11). The Word helps us fight better against the wiles of the devil. Besides, Satan also knows the Word. Jesus showed us that knowing the Word is crucial to defeating the enemy.

The Bible says that the devil tempted Jesus during His 40 days of fasting. Given that Jesus was hungry, the devil told Him to turn a stone into a loaf of bread if He was indeed the Son of God. Jesus replied that man should not live by bread alone but by every word that comes from the mouth of God (Luke 4:1–4). Jesus drew on Deuteronomy 8:3 to answer Satan.

Satan also offered the kingdoms of the earth in return for Jesus bowing down to him. Jesus countered, declaring what is written: that only the Lord is worthy of worship (Luke 4:8). We have just seen that, on two occasions, Jesus demonstrated great knowledge of the Word. The lesson to be learned herein is: if Jesus, who is God, demonstrated knowledge of the Word, we Christians are condemned to study the Word of God to live up to the persecutions of Satan. Furthermore, the power of the Word lies in its application.

Paul compares a Christian to a soldier whose sword is the Spirit, which is the Word of God (Ephesians 6:17). We can assert that this sword is sharper than any two-edged sword, penetrating to the point of splitting soul and spirit, joints and marrow, based on the effectiveness of the Word of God (Hebrews 4:12). The Word of God has the capacity to complement and arm us so that we are ready for every good deed. Satan is afraid of us when we battle him with the Word of God; therefore, let us use this weapon against him.

Today, many people think that the power of the Word is tainted by the excesses of false prophets who claim to proclaim the good news. The Word of God is not the fruit of human wisdom. The Bible has already warned us of these practices in the last days. Be assured that the power of the Word is the same yesterday, today, and forever, just like its author. However, it will have no effect unless we receive it with faith. The Word of God is powerful for those who believe. It will be effective if we open our hearts to faith. Bearing in mind what has just been said, the Holy Scriptures mention the skepticism of the people of Israel in Hebrews 4:2: "For this good news was preached to us as well as to them but the word that was preached to them did not profit them, because it did not find faith in those who heard it." This Bible verse proves that the Word of God must be coupled with faith if it is to produce results.

2.3. The Word of God: a Source of Prosperity

The Word is a key that opens the door to spiritual and material blessings. This means that our prosperity begins the moment we become actors in the Word of God. "Keep this Book of the Law always on your lips;

meditate on it day and night, so that you may be careful to do everything written in it. Then you will be prosperous and successful" (Joshua 1:8).

This Scripture shows us how God links our success to our commitment to His Word. If the Word of the Lord guides our actions, our success is inevitable. He who delights in the law of the Lord, meditating on it day and night, is like a tree whose leaves do not wither even in times of drought. He is a firmly planted tree. All his initiatives will succeed because he is linked to the source of life (Psalms 1:2–3). Christians are strongly advised to obey biblical principles if they want their projects to succeed (Luke 11:28).

2.4. The Word of God that Makes Us Wise

Fearing the Lord is the first step towards being wise (Psalms 111:10). Where does wisdom come from? It comes from the Word of God, which dwells among us abundantly and teaches us in all wisdom (Colossians 3:16). This Word also makes men wise unto salvation in the sense that it dictates the path to enter the Kingdom of God. Paul told Timothy that he knows the holy letters (the Word of God), which can make him wise to salvation through faith in Jesus Christ (2 Timothy 3:15). Through the Word of God, our capacity for judgment increases because we receive light (Psalms 119:130). It should also be pointed out that a life of holiness requires Christians to show wisdom towards their brothers and sisters.

2.5. The Word Matures the Christian

When babies are born, they need to be breastfed to live and grow. When you are born-again, you are a baby spiritually. The Word of God is the spiritual milk that makes a Christian grow. The Bible, therefore, says that we are like newborn babies who must drink pure spiritual milk to grow in salvation (1 Peter 2:2). Christians must make spiritual progress because it is more important than material progress.

You can change your house, car, and other furniture as you please, but know that your salvation depends on your spiritual progress. That is why we say that you must first work for your spiritual fulfillment. This progress must be remarkable.

Furthermore, the Word of God is not just milk but also bread to nourish our souls. We must consume His Word because it brings joy and gladness to our hearts (Jeremiah 15:16). Nowadays, people are much more interested in healing services than in Bible studies. Yet our prayers cannot be answered if they are not rooted in the Word of God.

A believer cannot live a life of sanctification without having matured spiritually. This means that being holy like the Lord Jesus is the guarantee of progress in Christ. James tells us that God has fashioned us according to His will, through the Word of truth, so that we might be the first fruits of His creatures (James 1:18). Depending on whether you have grown or stagnated spiritually, 2 options are possible. Either the Word of God keeps you away from sin, or you keep yourself away from the Word of God.

2.6. The Word of God Convinces

The Bible mentions that the Scriptures are inspired by God and are useful for convincing (2 Timothy 3:16). The Word of God enlightens us and guides our steps (Psalms 119:105). It is the Word that convinces us to forsake sin to live in holiness, for no one who is born of God will continue to sin because God's seed remains in them; they cannot go on sinning because they have been born of God (1 John 3:9).

We recall the biblical story of Saul, who did not respect God's commandments. Samuel used the Word of God to convince Saul that God hates greed, wickedness, and lies (1 Samuel 13:13). And the woman, who had several partners when she met Jesus, had gone to testify that she had just met a man who told her of her life story as if he had known her for a long time.

In doing so, she is about to be regenerated because the Word of Christ has convinced her. This is why the apostle Peter said that we have been regenerated by an incorruptible seed, which is the living and abiding Word of God (1 Peter 1:23). In other words, the Word convicts us, aiming to regenerate us.

2.7. The Word is a Source of Consolation

The Word is a source of solace when we are going through difficult times. Faced with the challenges of this world, we find hope when we are overwhelmed by the variations of life by meditating on the Word of God. Romans 15:4 says, "For everything that was written in the past was written to teach us, so that through the endurance taught in the Scriptures and the encouragement they provide we might have hope." This comfort can only be found in God's Word, knowing that His promises will never fail.

Thanks to the Word, we are not shaken even when we are in adversity. We have confident expectations. Paul advises us to have the hope of salvation as a helmet (1 Thessalonians 5:8). Make use of this helmet when depression is gnawing at you or when suicidal thoughts are on the verge of taking over the new person.

2.8. The Word of God Teaches and Instructs

The teaching and instructing function of the Word tends to transmit knowledge that should make us acceptable to God. This implies that when we begin to read and study the Word of God, we acquire solid knowledge about God Himself and His will. This is why we tend to think of well-educated people as Christians. When we follow the teachings of the Bible, we show restraint in word and deed.

The Word even teaches us how to choose our friends. The enemy of God must not be my friend. This attitude has nothing to do with a specific superiority complex. We are all God's creatures, but God's children agree to walk according to His will. As kind as a pagan may seem to you; he is an enemy because he is a soldier of the devil.

As Christians, we cannot be linked to pagans under any circumstances. Christian, in this case, means believer. He is not simply a person who confesses or acquiesces mentally. Obedience to the Word of God is the proof of belief, according to the Bible (1 John 2:3; 5:1–3). For demons also believe, but they do not do God's will.

If you do not obey the Word of God, you have a lack of belief (Romans 10:16–17). The term believer refers to a person who has experienced the plan of salvation (Acts 2:38). Furthermore, we cannot take pagans for friends because this leads to compromises with the world. Also, God exhorts us to separate ourselves from the world.

Some say they do not practice witchcraft; others say they do nothing wrong to be dubbed followers of Satan. People who support these ideas are wrong, because Jesus said, "He who is not with me is against me..." (Matthew 12:30).

Sometimes, people want us to explain our behavior as Christians. The best answer is to establish that the Word of God dictates Christian behavior. It is not government authorities, still less society. Those who do not allow themselves to be taught by the Word are like a car without brakes.

2.9. The Word Sanctifies and Purifies

To understand the power of the Word, think of someone who has not showered for 7 days. The smell of that body is undoubtedly unpleasant. Despite the smell, the person can change the situation by taking a bath. This is what the Word of God does. Jesus gave Himself up so we might be sanctified through the Word and purified through water baptism (Ephesians 5:25–26). This Word sanctifies us because it is the truth (John 17:17).

James likens those in whom the Word has no effect to a man who sees his true face in a mirror and then goes away and immediately forgets the shape of his natural face (James 1:23–24). We are talking here about our inner faces. In this sense, the Word of God shows us our true spiritual state. Under the impulsion of the Holy Spirit, the Word, above all else, sanctifies us and shows us what God can and wants to do with us.

Chapter 4:
The Shepherd's Role

A study of holiness must necessarily bring us into contact with the shepherd. The shepherd is responsible for looking after the sheep. Hence the role of church leaders. A leader is generally a person who can lead and influence to achieve an objective. In our case, the leader refers to someone whom God has placed at the head of a ministry.

1. Authority in the Church

At first glance, we must affirm that God created the governance of the Church. The Church is not simply a human organization, nor is it limited to one. It is the assembly of Christians who live in holiness and consecration while experiencing salvation. Being a member of an assembly of a particular denomination is not synonymous with salvation because salvation is personal. Nevertheless, the road to salvation is a collective one.

A Christian must not follow a leader who pushes one to act in contradiction with the teachings of the Bible, of his convictions if they are anchored in the Word of God, or who teaches false doctrine. When we speak of authority in the Church, it refers to the leaders that God has placed in ministries with the aim of leading his people on the path that leads to Heaven. This is what justifies organization in the Church.

The example of organization in the Church was given by Jesus. He chose twelve (12) disciples as His close collaborators, delegating to each one a particular mission. Judas was treasurer because he kept the purse (John 13:29). The book of Acts, which tells the story of the Church, highlights the administration, choice, and recognition of leaders, consistency in decision-making, and fellowship in the early Church.

2. The Early Church: An Organizational Model

The Bible tells us that one hundred and twenty people met to appoint another apostle after Judas had been hanged. They had set their sights on Joseph, called Barsabbas, nicknamed Justus, and Matthias. After praying, they finally chose Matthias (Acts 1:15–26). Verse 42 of the second chapter of the Book just quoted specifies that these people had persevered in the apostles' teaching, in fraternal communion, in the breaking of bread, and in prayer. This means that these believers recognized the leadership of the twelve in teaching doctrine and establishing fellowship. Regarding tithes and offerings, the Bible says that the apostles collected funds donated by the believers (Acts 4:35).

Furthermore, Acts 6 states that the 12 called a meeting of the disciples to set up a committee to look after the affairs of the Church, especially the widows. They chose 7 of them who were anointed with the Holy Spirit and wisdom (laying on of hands) so that the 12 could continue with the ministry of the Word and prayer. We also find in Galatians 2:11–14 Paul's rebukes to the Church leaders to refrain from false doctrines.

These examples illustrate that organization and authority run throughout the history of the Church of Christ. Each ministry and each assembly are under the protection of a shepherd whom God has appointed. It is, therefore, important that the assemblies have an administration responsible for making the work more efficient.

3. The Christian's Attitude towards the Leader

The authority of leaders in the Church stems from the Bible. Hebrews 13:17 states the following: "Have confidence in your leaders and submit to their authority, because they keep watch over you as those who must give an account. Do this so that their work will be a joy, not a burden, for that would be of no benefit to you." In addition, Paul tells us: "Now we ask you, brothers and sisters, to acknowledge those who work hard among you, who care for you in the Lord and who admonish you. Hold them in the highest regard in love because of their work. Live in peace with each other." (1 Thessalonians 5:12–13).

These Bible verses apply to all ministries and assemblies. In the light of these Scriptures, we must value the leaders of the Church by treating them with reverence because of the work they do. We do not respect and value them as men, but we value and fear the functions they perform. They may not be God, but they have received authority from God. We should respect them for that reason because the Word of God tells us: "For there is no authority except from God, and the authorities that exist have been instituted of God" (Romans 13:1). Verse 2 of the same Book speaks of the fate that awaits those who resist the order that God has established by opposing the authorities. Such people will bring condemnation upon themselves.

On the other hand, a servant of God who does not obey the voice of his shepherd or his leaders will face serious consequences. It is said that those who despise authority, who do not fear insulting glorious ones, will perish by their corruption and will thus receive the wages of their iniquity (2 Peter 2:10–13).

Similarly, Paul urges us to give double honor to elders who lead well, and especially to those involved in preaching and teaching (1 Timothy 5:17). He also said that the end of times will be marked, among other things, by a challenge to the authority established by God (2 Timothy 3:1–8). Jude tells us in verses 7 and 8 that the punishment of eternal fire will strike those who despise authority and insult glory.

In short, sanctification also requires respect for leaders in ministries and Christian assemblies. The Holy Scriptures highlight the need to value and honor people who have leadership positions because their power comes from God. With this attitude, we protect ourselves from the wrath of the Creator.

4. The Duties of a Good Leader

Leaders, whether they are pastors, teachers, evangelists, prophets, or deacons, must be examples to the world in general and to the members they lead in particular. The Bible says that whoever aspires to be an overseer desires a noble task (1 Timothy 3:1). Notice that the verse mentions a noble task. This means that leaders must be examples to follow in every sense of the word.

The leader of a Christian assembly must be above reproach. He must have only one wife because God hates adultery. He must also show proof of temperance and moderation, hospitality, be orderly in his conduct, and be apt to teach (1 Timothy 3:2).

God establishes spiritual criteria for choosing leaders. A man who does not run his house well cannot be a shepherd in the Church of Jesus Christ because it is impossible to care for the Church if he is not capable of managing his house. In addition, he must keep his offspring in obedience and perfect honesty. (1 Timothy 3:4–5).

5. A True Leader's Attitude

When God calls us to lead a Christian assembly or ministry, our first mission is to work for the Kingdom of God. However, some people who call themselves leaders seek stardom more than they focus on the Lord's work.

While God does not share His glory in any way, they are stubborn to the point of becoming puffed up with pride and megalomania. They only preach about financial prosperity. This is contrary to biblical advice.

The apostle John wanted Gaius to prosper in all respects and to be in good health, as the state of his soul prospered (3 John:1–2). In this part of the Scripture, the expression "in all respects" is of vital importance because it means that financial prosperity is of no importance if the state of the soul does not prosper in turn. For this reason, the leader must guide believers to live a life of holiness.

Consequently, the leader must show incorruptible probity because one can only give what one has. He must receive God's call.

5.1. God's Call

First, it is important to clarify that ministry is not a vocation that you choose for yourself by chance. It is God who must choose us. Thus, anyone considering a career in ministry must make sure that he has really received the Lord's call. God himself chooses his chosen ones. Some choose to respond to this noble call by submitting their whole lives to it, while others prefer to remain halfway by making this privilege a mere vocation. But ministry is not just a one-day call but a lifelong commitment.

Whoever wants to take charge of a ministry must have the certainty and conviction of having been called by God to minister. However, Satan sets up a whole series of tricks designed to limit or prevent us from having an impact on our world by making us constantly doubt the authenticity of our call.

There are many reasons why people pursue ministry. Some come out of altruism; they like to serve others. Others feel good when they are in a position of authority. These intentions are not bad, but they are not enough.

Some now come just to get money from believers who follow them on social media. For them, the ministry represents a good deal and a source of great wealth. Such motives are contrary to the very nature of the ministerial calling. However, there are legions of leaders who are driven by these bad intentions in Christian assemblies.

I went to a big city in the United States to organize a conference. The team and I went to see a pastor so that he could make the sanctuary available to us for several hours. I was stunned when I heard the demands the pastor made, which we thought were inconceivable for a man of God. As I left the temple, the voice of God told me to pronounce on this sanctuary whose leader had not been called. I raised my right hand and declared that this space was cursed because God was absent. Once said, once done! The sanctuary was closed by the authorities due to a set of embezzlements. This anecdote illustrates one thing: many people who call themselves leaders are not approved by God.

There is no exact way of defining the call to ministry. Each person receives the call according to their situation. Some have been called by revelation, while others have heard the voice of the Holy Spirit speaking to them. Nevertheless, those whom God has not called can be recognized by their deeds. They are not interested in the sanctification of God's people.

The Bible describes the different ways God calls His servants into the ministry. Abraham was 75 years old when God asked him to leave Harran and go to Canaan to receive the blessing that He had reserved for him (Genesis 12:1–5). The Word of God came to Ezekiel in the form of divine visions, and it was there that God's hand was upon him (Ezekiel 1:1–3), while Jesus asked Simon and Andrew to follow Him as they fished with their net (Matthew 4:18–19).

In short, the Bible describes a set of qualifications that ministers must demonstrate. Not everyone can be a leader. Leaders must maintain a lifestyle based on sanctification.

6. The Leader Against Sin

The leader, like all Christians, must flee from sin.

He has a responsibility to preach against sin. The Lord urged Ezekiel to warn the wicked and to speak to turn them from their wicked ways and save their lives. If the wicked man dies in his iniquity despite the warning, Ezekiel will save his soul. Otherwise, God will hold him accountable for the blood of the wicked (Ezekiel 3:18–19).

The leader must help people know what sin is by following the teachings of the Bible. He must guide believers along the path of holiness by establishing the necessary principles for maintaining a life of sanctification. These standards are for the people of God, especially the faithful, whose care the leader has before the Lord.

Furthermore, the true leader is a person who is filled with the Holy Spirit, and therefore, the Spirit of the Lord preaches through him (Joel 2:28). Since God hates sin, the leader must also hate sin. The Bible tells us that it is proof of love for God when we hate evil (Psalms 97:10). Furthermore, Proverbs 8:13 says that "the fear of the Lord is the hatred of evil." Thus, it is automatic to hate sin if we love God. Nevertheless, we must love the sinner. I keep saying that we must welcome the pagans whichever way they present themselves. Do not judge them; do not look at them with disdain. Whether they are homosexuals, drug users, or alcoholics, the Bible commands us to welcome them into the house of the Lord so that the Word of God can echo in them.

The leader is simply a messenger of God. He is not the author of the message. He must deliver the message without altering its content. If he fails to do so, he is in contravention of God.

Nonetheless, some leaders of the "feel good" gospel (see introduction) are so accommodating and hesitant that they can't preach against sin. It is also true that not all leaders have the same personalities, in the sense that some are more righteous and upright in their convictions than others. According to its leaders, preaching against sin does not reflect a genuine love for God's people. However, when you love someone who lives in sin, that does not mean you should not inform them that sin affects their salvation if they refuse to repent.

The leader who has received God's call preaches the truth regardless of people's feelings. The true preacher does not preach what people like to hear. If someone calls himself a leader and leaves God's people in sin, he deserves to be regenerated along with the sinful people.

7. The Tolerant and Cowardly Leader

The apostle John reports that the Son of God spoke to the angel (spiritual leader) of the Church of Thyatira in these words: "What I have against you is that you let..." (Revelation 2:18–20). The second part of this Scripture reflects a certain tolerance on the part of the leader of the Church of Thyatira. God cannot stand tolerant leaders.

No matter what a leader's inclinations may be, the Holy Spirit who dwells within him cannot tolerate sin. If the Holy Spirit reigns as King in his life, the Spirit's anointing and inspiration will give him the necessary strength not to tolerate sin.

The Bible's account of a servant of God named Eli is proof that God punishes leaders for their tolerance. In fact, Eli knew about the crimes committed by his sons, but he did nothing to stop them. The Lord told Samuel that the crime of the house of Eli would not be atoned for, neither with sacrifices nor with offerings (1 Samuel 3:13–14). Even towards his children, the leader must not be tolerant in the sense that he does nothing while being aware of the excesses.

Some leaders ignore the actions of their followers for fear that they will leave the assembly. I address these spiritual leaders to tell them that only the Holy Spirit is indispensable in a ministry. The leader himself can be replaced if he does not do God's will.

Others adopt this offhand behavior, attempting to always remain on the same wavelength with the Church committee, especially if these aberrations come from the members of the committee. A leader should not be motivated by a salary because he is, first and foremost, an employee of God. He is not like a company director whose mandate must be renewed regularly. No matter who is at fault, the leader must be uncompromising toward sin.

A leader's cowardice can also be seen in his courage to take a stand against evil under any conditions.

I witnessed a scene in an assembly where a sister said to a deacon that he should not feel comfortable handing out holy communion. The servant hammered that she had gone to the pastor to complain about the deacon, and the pastor did nothing in response. The leader of this congregation is a coward because he does not have the courage to sanction a deacon who lives a life of debauchery while pretending to work for God.

Sometimes, a worship service without musicians is better than one with musicians without the anointing. This is why we say that the leader must not be cowardly and tolerant of sin.

8. The Leader Must Avoid Demonic Activities

Mark tells the story of a man in the land of the Gadarenes who was possessed by unclean spirits. Having seen Jesus from a distance, the man rushed over and bowed down to him. It was not the man himself who bowed down, but rather the demons (Mark 5:6). This story supports the claim that demons possess some believers. For this reason, a leader worthy of the name needs to remain continually in prayer and fasting to fight the demons that want to take hold of them.

The forces of darkness can drive leaders away from God if they do not allow themselves to be led by the Holy Spirit, who lives within them. Of course, leaders are much more persecuted by Satan because they are placed at the head of a team working for God. Moreover, if the forces of darkness win the battle over a leader, it means that the Holy Spirit has not recognized his work. Therefore, God's anointing must constantly flow over him so that he does not fall into the devil's trap.

Furthermore, Satan is very persistent. When he tempted Jesus, he only left Him for a moment (Luke 4:13). Whenever we are faced with a demonic attack, we need to be aware of its persistent nature. We must counter it with determination. Satan will never give up as long as we are still alive on this earth.

Nevertheless, God gives us spiritual endurance so that we can withstand the devil's onslaught. A true leader must never stop fasting because the adversary prowls around all Christians, especially the Shepherd. Satan makes fleshly suggestions, but it is up to us to resist. The devil constantly urges us to succumb to the flesh. This is why leaders need to stay far away from demonic practices.

Conclusion

It is important to remember that God demands a life of holiness for our well-being, for the Bible says: "Our Fathers disciplined us for a little while as they thought best; but God disciplines us for our good, in order that we may share in his holiness" (Hebrews 12:10). At first sight, punishment is a source of sadness and anguish. However, we have the assurance in Christ that all things work together for the good of those who love the Creator, even when the situation we are in makes us feel uncomfortable (Romans 8:28).

Additionally, the first mission of a Christian on earth is to bear witness for Jesus by drawing inspiration from his life. This cannot be possible without a life of holiness because God Himself is eminently holy, and the Word refers to His absolute perfection and purity. Moreover, our salvation depends on it because sanctification is one of the acts of redemption.

Holiness is individual. Each person is individually responsible before God. Everyone must strive to live a life that pleases God to always be in a good relationship with Him.

Consequently, believers must set themselves apart for God, separating themselves from the world by dedicating their lives to the one who created them. This separation is necessary for the Holy Spirit to dwell in us. Jesus exhorted us to deny ourselves and take up our cross if we want to follow Him (Matthew 16:24).

Jesus pleased God in every way, obedient unto death (Philippians 2:8). In other words, he lived a holy and blameless life, not because he was never tempted or oppressed by Satan, the devil, but because he drew strength from perfect communion with the Father so as not to be shaken by the devil's repeated assaults.

However, in Jesus, two (2) natures coexisted: He was one hundred percent (100%) man and one hundred percent (100%) God. I draw your attention to the fact that Jesus had a human nature but not that of Adam, which is synonymous with a sinful nature.

Following the example of Jesus will not only lead us to a life of holiness but will also give us the strength to resist the evil spirits that drive us toward sin. Yet, no life of holiness can be envisioned without the presence of the Holy Spirit, who is an agent of sanctification for the whole being.

A life of sanctification also requires a life of submission and obedience to the Word of God, which will undoubtedly lead to a life of faith, without which we cannot fight against the wiles of the devil. The devil persecutes us mainly in three (3) ways: the lust of the flesh, the lust of the eyes, and pride.

The devil attempts to convince us that since we are in the flesh and the flesh is weak, we cannot have holy lives. He wants to persuade us that there is no way we can escape from daily sin. I will tell you again and again that the devil is a liar. The truth is that God has commanded us to be holy. Furthermore, our Savior Jesus condemned sin while in the flesh (Romans 8:3).

Leaders also have their share of responsibility. As shepherds, they will be held accountable for the sheep that God has entrusted to them. Leaders must honor their status as defenders of the Word of the Lord by encouraging God's people to practice a life of sanctification. They are simple messengers of God and must not, under any circumstances, preach tolerance for sin to gain the sympathy of sinners.

The life of sanctification does not mean that we are exempt from difficulties. If we must lose friends, jobs, and privileges of every kind to live a life of holiness, we must do so because God's love for us is priceless. Moreover, it would do a man no good to gain the whole world if he lost his soul (Matthew 16:26). Therefore, we must show our gratitude to

God and opt for salvation, no matter what surprises the world throws at us.

We must bear in mind that a life of holiness is not an unattainable dream. Knowing that he is the God who searches the heart and examines the mind (Jeremiah 17:10), if He has commanded us to be holy, He knows very well that we are capable of it.

To achieve this, Christians must allow themselves to be guided by the Holy Spirit by making faith their shield, by obeying the Word of God, by investing time in fasting and prayer, and by abstaining from all lusts. With this attitude, the believer will be true and sincere in the pursuit of holiness, knowing that, ultimately, the goal of sanctification is to be indeed like God.

Accordingly, we will live a life of holiness while fearing God, and we will await the return of Christ without anxiety.

Live the life of holiness!

Bibliography

David K. BERNARD, Loretta A. BERNARD, A la recherche de la sainteté (version électronique), 2017, 293 pages.

Joseph PRINCE, Spiritual warfare (electronic version), 2005, 80 pages.

Dag HEWARD-MILLS, Vaincre l'activité démoniaque (version électronique), 2008, 17 pages.

Dennis BURKE, Comment méditer la Parole de Dieu (version électronique), 30 pages.

Kenneth HAGIN, Conduit par l'Esprit de Dieu (version électronique), 79 pages.

Jason K. ALLEN, Discerning your call to ministry (version électronique), 217 pages.

Guy GOUJOU, Le chemin d'un fervent militant du royaume (version électronique), 103 pages.

Danie VERMEULEN, Comprendre le combat spirituel et les forteresses (version électronique), 53 pages.

Dallen GARRIS, 4 étapes pour un réveil spirituel (version électronique), 57 pages.

Yonggi D. CHO, La prière, clé du réveil (version électronique), 110 pages.

J. Heinrich ARNOLD, Discipleship (electronic version), 112 pages.

Rick WARREN, Une vie motivée par l'essentiel (version électronique), 131 pages.

Frank Hammond, Repercussions from sexual sins (electronic version), 47 pages.

La Bible du Semeur.

La Bible Thompson.

La Sainte Bible avec les commentaires de John MacArthur.

La Sainte Bible Esprit et Vie.

La Sainte Bible Scofield.

www.ingramcontent.com/pod-product-compliance
Lightning Source LLC
Chambersburg PA
CBHW060337130626
46553CB00003B/1033